PAST & PRESENT

EXETER

Hope you enjoy Exeter
as much as we have!
Kathleen D. Bailey

Opposite: The Powder House was built in 1771 to store gunpowder and weapons. Still the source of a "big bang," the town's annual fireworks are set off from this site. (Courtesy of Exeter Historical Society.)

EXETER

Kathleen D. Bailey and Sheila R. Bailey

From the time Benjamin F. Swiezynski picked up a camera, he focused it on his hometown, lovingly chronicling all aspects of Exeter life. He made a living at it, raising five children, but he also gave of his talent to his community. I knew him from my work as community news editor for the Exeter News-Letter, *and remember the well-dressed older man stopping by two or three times a week with an envelope of courtesy photographs. Not a lodge installation nor a ribbon-cutting went by without Ben shooting it. He showed free Halloween movies in the town hall, attached a loudspeaker to his station wagon to publicize Exeter events, was an enthusiastic communicant of St. Michael Church, and ensured a future for Seacoast students by advocating for the Region 10 Vocational Education Center, now the Seacoast School of Technology.*

This book is dedicated to Ben Swiezynski.

Library of Congress Control Number: 2021941630

Published by Arcadia Publishing
Charleston, South Carolina

Printed in the United States of America

For all general information, please contact Arcadia Publishing:
Telephone 843-853-2070
Fax 843-853-0044
E-mail sales@arcadiapublishing.com
For customer service and orders:
Toll-Free 1-888-313-2665

Visit us on the Internet at www.arcadiapublishing.com

On the Front Cover: The Major John Gilman House was built before the United States was even a country by one of early Exeter's prominent men for his son. Gilman descendants are still active in Exeter. (Present image, courtesy of Sheila R. Bailey; past image, courtesy of the Exeter Historical Society.)

On the Back Cover: This 1903 gem on the campus of Phillips Exeter Academy now houses the school's art department and Lamont Gallery, still serving students in the school's 240th year of operation. (Courtesy of the Exeter Historical Society.)

CONTENTS

ACKNOWLEDGMENTS

I am indebted to the Swiezynski family—Jim Swiezynski, Sandy Swiezynski Parks, Holly Swiezynski Jennejahn, and Benjamin F. "Skip" Swiezynski III—for sharing freely from their father's archives and for their many memories. We also honor their late sister, Carol Ann "Cas" Donovan, for her work with her father in their shop, and we honor Mary Swiezynski for keeping the home and raising five children so Ben could be Ben. Historic photographs taken by Benjamin F. Swiezynski and courtesy of the Swiezynski family are noted as (BFS).

The Exeter Historical Society shared photographs, reference materials, and advice. Special thanks go to curator Barbara Rimkunas and volunteer Pam Gjettum. Whenever I had a question someone could not answer they would say, "Have you talked to Barbara?" I did, and she knew. Richard Cole, Vicki Lukas, and Willie Gustafson also assisted in tracking down elusive facts. Images from the historical society's collection are noted as (EHS).

Additional thanks go to Lara Bricker for her interview in the *Exeter News-Letter* and for introducing me to "You Know You're From Exeter When…"; Bert Freedman for material on Woolworth's; Alma Hall for an afternoon of reminiscences; Bob Hall for railroad references; Exeter Community Television and Robert Glowacky; Norma "Teddie" Smith and Sandy Smith for access to their material; Thomas Tufts for fire information; Elizabeth Griswold Vershay for photographs and memories; Daniel Cartier for images; Emma Stratton and the American Independence Museum; Darren Winham and Exeter Economic Development; the Exeter Select Board and town manager Russ Dean; Keith Vincent, operator of the Courthouse History blog; Pam Hallett, Exeter First Baptist Church, and her material on the Star Window, quoting from *Our Christian Symbols* by Friedrich Rest, published in 1954; Rebekah Welch and Inn at the Bandstand; Carol Walker Aten, author of *Postcards from Exeter*, published in 2003; the many residents and former residents who encouraged me through "You Know You're From Exeter When…"; and the Historic American Buildings Survey (HABS), Library of Congress.

Unless otherwise stated, all modern images were shot by my daughter Sheila R. Bailey.

INTRODUCTION

My family and I are honorary Exonians, driving over from our Raymond base to shop, dine, or attend events such as the UFO Festival and the Festival of Trees. We've done research at the library and frozen our toes at the Holiday Parade. We've strolled Swasey Parkway for the summer Farmers' Market and ducked inside Exeter High School on a freezing February morning for the Seacoast Growers' Winter Farmers' Market.

In Exeter, I often have the same feeling I experience at Lexington and Concord. When I stand on the Lexington Green, I know a sense of awe as I watch people walk dogs and babies, throw Frisbees, or read a book. History happened here, and people live their normal lives right in the middle of it. It gives me chills.

I get the same feeling in Exeter (albeit less bloody). High school kids walking home from school pass by places where Washington ate, Lincoln slept, and the Republican Party was a gleam in Amos Tuck's eye. Young moms with strollers walk by the homes or academy dorms of men who would go on to change their world. Mill workers, old money, an expat to Paris who chronicled World War I for the folks at home. They lived their lives in a place where history happened.

Betsy Griswold Vershay knew she lived in a historic building, the Tenney House, but it didn't faze her nor her three sisters. They roller-skated in the basement, dried their hair on the front steps, and at least one Christmas, threw snowballs from the classic third-story pediment, prompting a call from a neighbor to their mother.

Exeter kids put the bleachers on the roof of the high school for a senior prank and drove through town on the back of a flatbed whenever the Blue Hawks won a football championship. In the town hall where Abraham Lincoln spoke, they gathered on Halloween to watch cartoons and a variety show coordinated by local photographer Benjamin Swiezynski. They saw Santa arrive on a fire truck and whispered their wishes to him in the gazebo donated by Ambrose Swasey, an Exeter boy whose influence spread across the country.

Exeter was also a microcosm of New England life, with social strata including Phillips Exeter Academy, millworkers, small-town shopkeepers, and civil servants. Alma Hall, a native, told me how in her youth there were "shoe factory people" and "textile mill people" and how they lived in the respective ends of town where their employment was and rarely interacted. Mill life wasn't enough for Hall or her late husband, Robert, so they carved out a career with their own variety store, working 12-hour days 52 weeks a year "until I put my foot down," Hall said. "Then we took a week's vacation."

In the 20th century, two forces dominated Exeter life: Phillips Exeter Academy, the renowned preparatory school, and the Exeter Manufacturing Company. The Kent family, owners of the cotton mill, put their stamp on everything from a fabric store to the local bank.

"Town and Gown" were "townier" and "gownier," according to Betsy Griswold Vershay, whose father worked at the academy for most of his career. While the academy was off-limits to girls, she and her sisters attended a private elementary school and rarely interacted with the "town" kids. The dynamic changed after the 1970s, with day-student options, more scholarships for local kids, and the welcoming of female students.

In my work with the *Exeter News-Letter*, I received many of Ben Swiezynski's courtesy photographs and spoke with him on an almost weekly basis. The man who arrived with an envelope of crisp black-and-white prints was known to everyone as "Ben." I was fortunate to have what may have been the last newspaper interview with Ben, who spoke about topics ranging from the war to his Catholic faith to vocational education. (He was instrumental in starting the Seacoast School of Technology). In conversation, he mentioned that "downtown," the Water Street commercial district, hadn't changed much physically since his youth. The businesses changed and moved out, hardware stores giving way to boutiques and gift shops and shoe stores replaced by spas. But the buildings themselves, the redbrick facades, remained the same.

The town made some early mistakes, allowing the Folsom Tavern to be turned into a trolley waiting room. St. Michael Parish sold its Gothic brick building on Center Street, constructing a more modern house of worship on the corner of Front and Lincoln Streets, with the old church replaced by a bank. Rockingham County sold its crenelated Victorian courthouse to another bank, moving to a modern building on Hampton Road and then to a complex in Brentwood. But the courthouse and historic preservation may have had the last laugh: the bank occupying the old courthouse lot closed its drive-through in 2019, citing changing consumer patterns.

In the 1940s, 1950s, and 1960s, Water Street was everything to Exeter. Residents shopped for hardware, groceries, and school clothes in their beloved downtown, often at locally owned shops such as Chet's, Abbots', or the Curtain Shop. Mothers either didn't drive or relinquished the family car to Dad for work, so they were dependent on downtown for household needs. Children walked to the IOKA on Saturday afternoon or to a corner store to spend their precious dimes. Downtown may not have had everything they wanted, but it had everything they needed.

The picture changed with the advent of department stores, supermarkets, and other chain retailers in the 1960s and 1970s. Exeter experienced some urban sprawl, notably down Portsmouth Avenue, but it worked out for the best for the growing town. Residents had their options expanded, while downtown remained downtown.

And downtown is enjoying its second golden age, with boutiques and antiques, unique restaurants and artisan chocolate, and an independent bookstore, making Exeter the stroll of choice on a lazy afternoon. Festivals celebrating everything from the American Revolution to UFO sightings draw visitors to a classic New England village.

The consumers change, the Colonial and Federal and Victorian buildings endure, with stories to tell to anyone who will listen.

I realized Ben was right. One doesn't see a lot of wrecking balls in Exeter. Since townspeople rose up to save the Sleeper House back in the 1970s, the theme has been recycling rather than rubble, with classic homes and storefronts being put to new use. Even a Pizza Hut and a Friendly's on Portsmouth Avenue have been revamped into a brewhouse and a diner. Locally owned, of course.

It's a good way to be.

—Kathleen Bailey, 2020

CHAPTER 1

A BRAVE
NEW WORLD

The Giddings Tavern at Park and Summer Streets had its origins in May 1729 when Thomas Webster conveyed a deed of "house lott and garden" to his daughter Deborah, wife of Zebulan Giddings. The house, expanded and restored over the years, is privately occupied and was one of the Exeter buildings selected for the Historic American Buildings Survey, a project of the WPA during the Great Depression. (HABS.)

In 1709, councilor John Gilman was not taking any chances. He built his house with a number of defensive features, including small windows for firing through, an overhang with firing holes in the floor, and the mechanism for a wooden portcullis, if necessary. The Gilman Garrison House, owned by Historic New England, was listed in the National Register of Historic Places in 1976. (BFS.)

A BRAVE NEW WORLD

This house at 16 Epping Road, built in 1676, is also an example of a "garrison," or fortified home. It has a steep pitched roof and asymmetrical facade. Built as an ordinary house, it was later fortified for defense. The house was modernized in 1911, though later owners have worked to restore it to its early style. It was listed in the National Register of Historic Places in 1980. (EHS.)

This house off Epping Road represents the transition from Georgian to Federal style and was built by Nathaniel Conner, a master builder, in the early 1800s. It was significantly remodeled in 1895 by descendant Arthur Conner. While the house is privately occupied, the 235-acre grounds are a wildlife management area managed by New Hampshire Fish and Game. The property represents 300 years of Exeter history, qualifying it for the National Register of Historic Places. (HABS.)

The people who birthed this nation knew they were doing something momentous, and often named their children accordingly. Dorothy Bartlett and Eliphalet Hale christened their first daughter Liberty. She married Richard Emery, and they had one daughter, Catherine Hale Emery. The girl named for freedom lived to see her young nation survive the War of 1812 and died in February 1829 at the age of 62. The Liberty Emery House at 41 Main Street is now privately occupied. (EHS.)

Col. Samuel Folsom's tavern, built in 1775, hosted George Washington, among other notables. The Society of the Cincinnati, a fraternal organization started in 1793 for Continental officers, acquired the building, moving it to their property on Spring Street. Foster and Martha Stearns restored it. The building is now part of the American Independence Museum and is used for special events. It is shown in 1973. (BFS.)

The Ladd-Gilman House, built in 1721, was occupied by a New Hampshire governor, state treasurer, and several other of the young country's notables. The Society of the Cincinnati purchased the house in 1902. In 1985, a workman discovered a Dunlap Broadside, one of the original copies of the Declaration of Independence, in the attic, and the house entered its second life as the American Independence Museum. It is shown in 1960. (BFS.)

Shown in 1959, the unique curved building at the junction of Water and Chestnut Streets is attributed to Jonathan Folsom of Portsmouth (1785–1825) for Simeon Folsom, an Exeter nail-maker. It went through several iterations, including a major renovation in 2014 by Merrimack Design. It also extends the Lincoln connection for Exeter: Robert Lincoln boarded here while at Phillips Exeter Academy, and his father dined here with his son on his acclaimed 1860 visit. (BFS.)

The Perry-Dudley House at 14 Front Street, built between 1805 and 1813, is considered one of Exeter's finest examples of Federal architecture. It was built for Dr. William Perry, a leading physician of the time, succeeded in his role by his son William Gilman Perry. Currently an office building, it was listed in the National Register on June 21, 1971. (EHS.)

The first in the trio of antique yellow houses anchoring Front Street was built by George Sullivan in 1809. The Sleeper family purchased the home in 1885. The property was the focus of an early historic preservation protest in 1970, when residents gathered to object to the house being torn down and replaced with a bank. While banks prevailed over other classic buildings, the Sleeper House stayed and today is a popular bed-and-breakfast. (EHS.)

The Gardner House, at 12 Front Street, was the birthplace of Elizabeth Jane (Gardner) Bougereau. Born in 1837, she studied drawing and painting at Lasell Seminary. After the Civil War, she moved to Paris for further study, married her art instructor, and remained there. Through letters, she gave Exeter a front-row seat to World War I. The house is now part of the Front Street Historic District, listed in the National Register of Historic Places. (EHS.)

Nathaniel Gilman sold the property that was to become 79 Front Street to John Rogers for $300 in 1818. The house, shown here with a proper Victorian gentleman standing in front, has always been privately occupied. (EHS.)

Another home occupied by the notable Gilman family, this Front Street house was built by Dr. Dudley Odlin in 1735 and owned in succession by Nathaniel Gilman, his son Joseph Taylor Gilman, and Joseph's widow Mary, who married Charles Bell, governor of New Hampshire from 1881 to 1883. The property, purchased by Phillips Exeter Academy in 1909, now houses the academy's offices for alumni relations and development. (EHS.)

When Capt. Epes Ellery retired from the sea, he first built a home on Linden Street, a mile from the center of Exeter. Deciding that his area was "too quiet," he had the house moved to Front Street. In 1860, Mrs. James Bell, a widow, occupied the house with her two daughters. Purchased by Phillips Exeter Academy in 1945, the building at 60 Front Street is currently used as the academy's admissions office. (EHS.)

The Maj. John Gilman House at 25 Cass Street is one of three remaining examples of a Georgian gambrel-roofed house. It was built in 1738 by local businessman John Gilman, of the Gilman Garrison House, for his son and namesake. The home underwent an extensive restoration in the 1960s and was listed in the National Register of Historic Places in 1988. It is now privately occupied. (EHS.)

Even Exeter did not always get it right. The Rundlett-Boardman House at 20 Front Street was razed in 1971 and replaced with a park, the Town House Common. Though the town had voted to form a Historic District Commission the year before, it was too late for the Rundlett-Boardman House. But the Town House Common, seen here in fall splendor, gave residents one more place to relax downtown and still beats a gas station any day. (EHS.)

Lewis Cass (1782–1866) was born in this house on Cass Street, but his influence extended across the country. He was a senator from Michigan, ran for president twice, and served as Andrew Jackson's secretary of war and James Buchanan's secretary of state. He was a supporter of states' rights, or "popular sovereignty," leading up to the Civil War. The house is currently privately occupied. (EHS.)

Starting in 1818, printer John Williams and his brother Benjamin ran a publishing company that employed 50 people and produced 50,000 bound books each year. Williams built this brick house on Front Street in 1828, and his brother built a similar Greek Revival home on Ladd's Lane. Exeter became a publishing center for New Hampshire, with eight publishing houses at one point. The home is now privately occupied. (EHS.)

CENTURY OF PROGRESS

The Moses-Kent House, at 1 Pine Street, was built in 1868 by Henry Clay Moses, a prominent wool merchant. He purchased two lots totaling five acres and built a Second Empire–style home with three stories, a mansard roof, and a tower. In 1901–1902, it underwent alterations by purchaser George Kent, owner of the Exeter Manufacturing Company. The house, now privately occupied, was listed in the National Register in September 1985. (BFS.)

The Merrill Building, at 163 Water Street, is a three-story Italianate commercial block built in 1874 with enough corbels, pediments, and ornamentation to satisfy any Victorian. It was built by Charles Merrill, a pharmacist. William Seward purchased the building in 1927 and ran Seward's Drug Store, a gathering place for local youths, until his retirement in 1944. (BFS.)

The Granite State Bank, ironically made of brick, took shape at 27 Front Street in 1831. The substantial building had a second-floor apartment for the cashier. The building later housed the Exeter Historical Society and is now home to a variety of shops and offices. (EHS.)

The small building attached to Exeter's historic Sleeper House was built in 1910 and was operated for many years by the Sleeper family as a jewelry store. Otis Sleeper purchased the house in 1889, adding the outbuilding seven years later. Sleepers' operated for more than 60 years. The building went through several iterations before its current one, the Otis. restaurant. Otis. serves modern American cuisine with an emphasis on fresh ingredients from local farms. (EHS.)

This building housed three generations of pharmacies, beginning when A.S. Wetherell built it and opened his drugstore in 1896. It was later the home of Thompson's Drug, then Styles Rexall Drug from 1957 to 1989. Geoff and Liz Pendexter's Whirlygigs Toy Shop now occupies the space and serves Exeter and the surrounding communities with quality toys in an Old World setting. (EHS.)

Amos Tuck lived at 89 Front Street in this Italianate Revival home. In February 1945, Tuck called together 263 anti-slavery colleagues at First Parish Church to suggest forming an abolition party, the Independent Democrats, who eventually became the Republican Party. In his spare time, Tuck was an attorney, congressman, Lincoln delegate to the 1860 Republican convention, developer of railroads in the West, and trustee of Phillips Exeter Academy. The home is now privately owned. (EHS.)

Amos Tuck's first home in Exeter was this house at 72 Front Street. He bought it, renovated it, and lived there from 1840 to 1843. His son Edward Tuck was born there. Edward would go on to make a name for himself as a financier and philanthropist, engineering the naming of Exeter's new boys' high school after his father. After Exeter High School moved to a new facility on Route 27, the complex, housing School Administrative Unit (SAU) 16, Exeter Adult Education, and the Seacoast School of Technology, returned to its "Tuck" name. (EHS.)

There has been a public building on this site since 1838, when the original Swampscott Hotel burned. A year later, the Squamscott Hotel was built. In 1853, it was one of the sites where Amos Tuck met with like minds to formulate what would become the Republican Party. It has been a Phillips Exeter Academy dorm and housed SAU 16, and is now an office building named after Maj. Abraham Blake, an early proprietor. (EHS.)

In 1932, academy alumnus William Boyce Thompson left money in his will for the building of the Exeter Inn, a classic New England hotel in the heart of Exeter. The inn belonged to the school for its first 75 years and was transferred to a leasing company, Someplaces Different, in 1997. The inn boasts memorabilia from William P. Chadwick, the original owner of the land, including a spar from his ship the *Sunbeam*. (EHS.)

Ambrose Swasey (1846–1937) never forgot his hometown. He trained as a mechanical engineer and migrated to Cleveland, Ohio, where he earned a name in his field, serving as president of the American Society of Mechanical Engineers (1904–1905). An amateur astronomer, he built astronomy equipment and had a crater on the moon named after him. In 1929, Swasey donated the funds to create the Exeter Shore Parkway, later renamed Swasey Parkway in his honor. (EHS.)

Swasey is also responsible for the bandstand in the center of town, which hosts everything from concerts by the Exeter Brass Band to Santa's arrival on a fire truck. The town had a previous wooden bandstand, but by the early 1900s, it was in poor shape. Swasey offered to fund a new one, and the town accepted. The bandstand was dedicated on August 10, 1916, followed by an Exeter Brass Band concert. (EHS.)

Henry Shute, a Phillips Exeter alumnus, Harvard graduate, and judge, parlayed his Exeter boyhood into a Tom Sawyer–like series of stories, the best known of which is *The Real Diary of a Real Boy*. His home on Pine Street is now privately occupied. (BFS.)

CHAPTER 3

WHERE WE WORSHIP

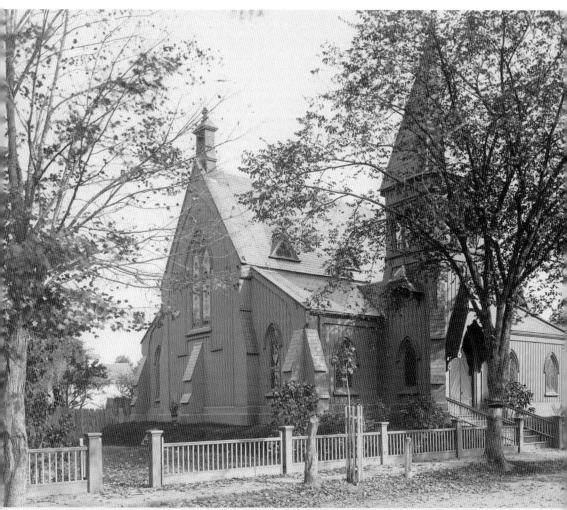

Christ Episcopal Church was birthed on Christmas Day 1864, when three Phillips Exeter Academy students walked eight miles to attend Christmas services at an Episcopal church in Epping. The following year, an Episcopal congregation was organized, and a Carpenter Gothic building was erected on Elliott Street. The building served the congregation well but began to show its age in the mid-20th century. A new building, futuristic in style, was erected on Pine Street. (EHS.)

The Congregational Church in Exeter was first formed in 1638 by the town's founder, Rev. John Wheelwright. Expelled from the Massachusetts Bay Colony, Wheelwright decided to try his luck farther north, and his luck held. The congregation moved into the current building in 1798, and it has remained a house of worship ever since. The church retains its classic style while moving with the times, embracing the LGBT community and partnering with a congregation in Zimbabwe. (EHS.)

Phillips Church, at the corner of Front Street and Tan Lane, has been a spiritual beacon for academy students, faculty, and the community since 1897, when it was designed by Cram, Goodhue & Ferguson of New York City. Ralph Adams Cram, a native of Hampton Falls, also designed other academy structures. The school shared the building with the First and Second Congregational Churches until 1922, when it became full owner. (Courtesy of Teddie Smith.)

Phillips Church, Exeter, N. H.

St. Michael Church began as a mission in 1848, administered by the Immaculate Conception Church of Lawrence, Massachusetts. Its first building went up in 1879 on Center Street. A school, St. Michael School, operated from 1932 to 1972. The school building was recycled into Exeter's Main Street School. The parish moved to Lincoln Street in 1958. The original St. Michael was torn down and replaced by a bank, as seen above. (BFS.)

The "new" St. Michael Church is shown during construction. While locals have bemoaned the destruction of the Gothic beauty on Center Street, the streamlined design of the new church on Front and Lincoln Streets has met area Catholics' needs well into the 21st century. (BFS.)

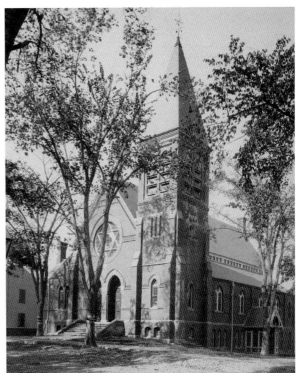

Exeter's Baptist congregation built its first small meetinghouse on Water Street in 1834. In 40 years, the growing congregation recognized a need for more space and built the redbrick church at 2 Spring Street, which became its permanent home. Peabody and Stearns of Boston were the architects, and the first service was held on February 20, 1876. The church is notable for the stained-glass window in the shape of a six-pointed star. The building was recently sold. (EHS.)

WHERE WE WORSHIP

This building on Elm Street was originally built by the Second Parish Congregational Church and called the Elm Street Chapel. It was successively home to the Advent Christian Church, Calvary Baptist Church, and eventually Faith Lutheran Church, which still operates under the name of ReGeneration Church. (BFS.)

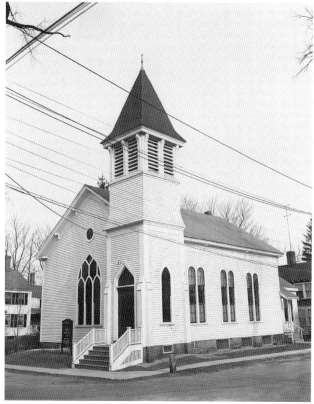

The church on the corner of Front and Center Streets was built in 1845 and first occupied by Exeter's Universalist congregation. In 1867, the Universalists, now merged with the Unitarians, sold the building to the United Methodists. The Methodist congregation built a modern building on Route 27 in 1996 and sold the now historic church to the local Presbyterian congregation, which stayed until a four-alarm fire destroyed the structure in November 2003. The spot is currently a vacant lot. (Right, BFS; below, EHS.)

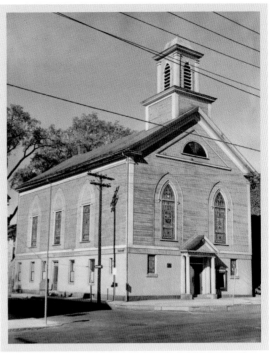

Advent Church, Unitarian Church and Parsonage, Exeter, N. H.

The Gothic Revival church designed by Ware and Van Brunt in 1868 served the Unitarian/Universalist Society on Elm Street for nearly 100 years. An addition, Unity Hall, was constructed in the summer and fall of 1890. In 1942, the wartime economy made it necessary to raze the original church, and the congregation remodeled Unity Hall as their sanctuary. The current congregation is working with Merrimack Design to equip the building for the future. (Courtesy of Teddie Smith.)

This Winter Street building has hosted several different aspects of Exeter life: the Winter Street School, Rockingham Furniture, the Knights of Columbus Hall, and most recently, Exeter Presbyterian Church after the 2003 fire destroyed its historic building. (BFS.)

CHAPTER 4

CIVIC LIFE AND GOVERNMENT

Exeter Hospital started in 1896 as a small cottage hospital on Pine Street in Exeter. The hospital moved to a campus off High Street and continued growing. It now has approximately 2,300 employees, more than 400 affiliated physicians, more than 5,200 annual admissions, and approximately 31,000 visits to its emergency department. (EHS.)

In 1855, a new town hall was constructed to replace a "town house" on Court Street. The cost was $30,000, and Rockingham County put in $8,000 so it could also house county offices and the court. The building hosted town meetings and a future president, Abraham Lincoln, in 1860. The town hall continues to function as a venue for everything from the Chamber Children's Fund Festival of Trees to forums at the UFO Festival. (EHS.)

In 1963, Rockingham County's government moved to a new facility on Hampton Road in Exeter. The move freed up space in the county's former Records Building at 10 Front Street. After extensive discussion in 1964 and 1965, the town purchased 10 Front Street and moved its municipal functions from the town hall to the newly-christened town office building. (EHS.)

This impressive brick building, built in 1893, served as the county courthouse until 1963, when both the courthouse and the county records functions moved to Hampton Road. The building was demolished, one of the few times in Exeter history that a structure was not recycled, and the Exeter Banking Co. bought the property for its drive-through. Exeter Banking was later acquired by Citizens Bank, and the drive-through was shuttered in 2019, though an ATM remains. (BFS.)

CIVIC LIFE AND GOVERNMENT

In 1963, this building on Hampton Road perfectly suited a growing county and Seacoast area. It served as the county seat until 1997, when county operations moved to Brentwood. Designed by Maurice Witmer, it is currently occupied by medical offices. (BFS.)

Exeter had a voluntary fire society as early as 1798. By 1873 there were four stations, on Main Street at the foot of Town Hill, on Front Street at the tracks, on Epping Road, and this redbrick classic on Water Street. The station was active until the 1950s, when functions were consolidated on Court Street. It was later developed into the Green Bean, a popular lunch spot. (EHS.)

CIVIC LIFE AND GOVERNMENT

As the town grew, so did the firefighting force, and services were consolidated in the 1950s at a new building on Court Street. But Exeter's needs soon outgrew the station. In 1979, public safety functions moved into the Municipal Complex at the corner of Court and Bow Streets. But the last call was not sounded for the Court Street station: it now houses the Exeter Senior Center and the Exeter Fire Museum. (BFS.)

In 1886, the town appropriated $15,000 for a new library. The result was this small but elegant building with a central rotunda and reading rooms branching off to either side. Finished in 1894, it was dedicated to the town's Civil War veterans. But Exeter's readers gradually outgrew the space. In 1987, a new library opened on Chestnut Street. The Exeter Historical Society took over the Front Street building, continuing to educate the public. (BFS.)

This stately building on Court Street served first as Exeter High School for boys, then as the Court Street Elementary School, and most recently as the Recreation Center. (BFS.)

The post office on Front Street has served Exeter since 1931. Its gracious proportions and design fit in with the historic homes and businesses in the downtown area. (Courtesy of Teddie Smith.)

Post Office, Exeter, N. H.

CIVIC LIFE AND GOVERNMENT

CHAPTER 5

DOWNTOWN
DELIGHTS

The Court Street Market, affectionately called "Gerrio's," was part of a network of small corner-store groceries serving kids with penny candy and housewives who either did not drive or turned the family car over to their husbands on workdays. The Court Street Market was demolished to make way for the Safety Complex in 1979. (Dan Cartier.)

Water Street in the 1950s and 1960s was a hub of activity, providing Exonians with just about everything they needed, from ball gowns to ball-peen hammers. The parking meters were torn out in the spring of 1973, allowing the growing number of specialty shops to advertise free parking and enhance the Exeter experience. (BFS.)

DOWNTOWN DELIGHTS

The Goodwin Block housed a number of businesses, including Irma's Cafe, Foy Insurance, and at least one iteration of Ben's Foto Shop. It was razed in 1970 and replaced by another building. In 2007, the Squamscott Block was built and fed the need for downtown housing with luxury apartments above and businesses on the first floor. (BFS.)

Dick and Mary Manix owned Chet's, a men's and boys' clothing store, at 231 Water Street in the 1960s and 1970s, joining other independent clothing stores such as the Colony Shop and Abbot's. The building was later occupied by two coffee shops: Cecelia's and the current St. Anthony's Bakery. (BFS.)

Samson's Market operated in the McReel Building and was one of several downtown groceries, including the Exeter Food Market and an early iteration of the A&P. Current occupants include specialty shops, offices, and an ice-cream shop patronized before or after a stroll down Swasey Parkway. (BFS.)

Built in 1915, Exeter's IOKA Theater witnessed the evolution of the talkie, Dish Night during the Depression, morale-boosting 1940s newsreels, and a changing world. It was the scene of first dates and first dreams. But the rise of the automobile and other entertainment drew Exeter youth out of town. The IOKA showed its last film, *Miracle on 34th Street*, in 2008. Recently purchased, the building will be converted for condos and businesses. (BFS.)

The Freedman family purchased the Smith Block in 1925, and it became the home for F. W. Woolworth's, the premier five-and-dime in the 1940s, 1950s, and 1960s. But Woolworth's closed in the 1990s due to changing consumer habits, and Bert Freedman moved his sports supply store George & Phillips into a portion of the building, adding locally-made gifts to the mix. He recently announced another move for his century-old business. (BFS.)

In the 1960s and 1970s, Exeter began to sprawl, with larger stores carving out spots from farmland on generous Portsmouth Avenue. Globe, Exeter's first modern department store, opened in 1970. The "strip" has become a mecca for chain stores and car dealerships, helping to keep downtown pristine and postcard-ready. (BFS.)

DOWNTOWN DELIGHTS

Paquette's, Exeter's first modern supermarket, offered, according to a 1954 *Exeter News-Letter* account, "conveyor belts on cashier counters operated by a foot lever. Popular music will be brought to the ears of shoppers by means of a high fidelity recording set." The store relocated to Portsmouth Avenue, offering free parking for customers' finned cars, and was renamed Champagne's. The plaza now hosts a number of small businesses, including this gourmet grocery. (BFS.)

In the 1940s, 1950s, and 1960s, America ran on Sears-Roebuck, the department-store chain famous for its mail-order catalogs. Exeter had a small Sears catalog store on the corner of Water Street and the String Bridge. But Sears, and its beloved catalog, fell victim to changing consumer trends. The building was later occupied by Lopardo's Jewelry and several real estate firms. (BFS.)

Abbot's, at 145 Water Street, provided "quality infants' and children's apparel," according to a 1960s chamber of commerce booklet. Abbot's shared a building with Moana's Lunch, one of several grassroots diners, including Irma's Cafe, Kurtz's, and the lunch counter at Woolworth's. Downtown continues to support locally and regionally based restaurants, while a quick bite can be obtained from the chain eateries on Portsmouth Avenue. (BFS.)

This building next to Swasey Parkway and the academy boat ramp housed the administrative functions of the Exeter and Hampton Electric Company for many years after its former building at 81–83 Water Street was deemed too crowded for a growing company. The utility merged with Concord Electric in 2002 and reopened as Unitil. The Water Street building has since been used as business offices and an art gallery. (BFS.)

The Great Atlantic and Pacific Tea Company took a share of the Exeter market early on, with a small A&P store next to an early version of Woolworth's. It later expanded to this space on Portsmouth Avenue. The popular Rogan's Coffee Shop replaced it for several years, and the site is now the home of Aroma Joe's. (BFS.)

The First National store started on Water Street but moved to growing Portsmouth Avenue, serving the needs of the 1950s homemaker with plenty of free parking and plenty of choices. It was part of the growing sprawl down the formerly rural road, but the extension to Portsmouth Avenue freed up downtown to do what it does best: specialty shops with a generous helping of charm. (BFS.)

Bomze Furniture and Appliances served Exeter's home goods needs on the rapidly expanding Portsmouth Avenue. Bomze provided local homeowners with the latest in Mid-century furniture, exemplified by its own futuristic building. The site is now occupied by Sanel Auto Parts. (BFS.)

Along with grocery stores, hardware stores were a fixture on Water Street in the 1940s, 1950s, and 1960s. Before Home Depot and Lowe's, a man who might be your neighbor or go to your church served up your home improvement needs, along with advice both solicited and unsolicited. The former Village Paint building is now occupied by a Thai restaurant. (BFS.)

The Exeter Banking Company opened on Water Street in 1893. It merged with First NH Bank in 1991 and changed its name to Citizens Bank in 1996. The company has flowed with the times, compressing its Victorian-style lobby to two teller stands and closing its drive-through with the rise of online banking. (BFS.)

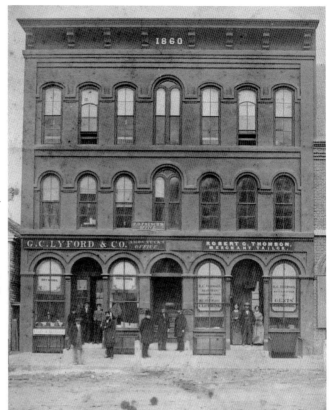

The Exeter Dry Goods store proudly occupied this spot in the late 1800s. The Rockingham National Bank set up shop in Exeter in 1926. It merged with Indian Head in 1972 and subsequently with Fleet Bank in 2000. While the building remains much the same, the spot at 97 Water Street is now occupied by the Capital Thai restaurant, one of many downtown dining options. (BFS.)

CHAPTER 6

EDUCATION

Exeter native William Robinson, born in 1793, died in Georgia, but not before bequeathing a sum of money to Exeter for the purpose of educating young women. The town built a grand Second Empire edifice complete with a cupola, and it ran for 86 years. But changing times and a crumbling building moved the town toward coeducation, and in the fall of 1956, the girls joined the boys at Exeter High School. The old building burned in October 1961. (BFS)

Tuck High School, established in 1848, served the young men of the community from its location on Court Street until 1912, when it moved to Linden Street. In 1956, it merged with Robinson Female Academy and went coeducational. Exeter High School moved to Route 27 in 2006. The Linden Street site now houses SAU 16, Exeter Adult Education, and Seacoast School of Technology, returning to its roots as the Tuck Learning Center. (Courtesy of Teddie Smith.)

Tuck High School, Exeter, N. H.

Even in a history-rich town, the senior prank is a tradition burnished by time. Sandy Swiezynski Parks remembers when the class of 1968 managed to maneuver a set of bleachers to the top of the old EHS annex. She is not sure, or not telling, how they got them back down. Below is the annex, now part of the Tuck Learning Center, sans bleachers. (BFS.)

This building, Exeter Area Junior High School, educated the middle-grade students of SAU 16 from 1977 to 1998, when the Cooperative Middle School was built. The area's youths are still served, as the Southern District YMCA bought the site and built its own facility. (BFS.)

From its beginning in 1848, St. Michael Parish sought to educate local Catholics. It opened its own school on Main Street in 1932. The school closed in 1972 and was purchased by the Exeter School District to house its lower grades as the Main Street School. Religious education continues in Michael House, the congregation's parish house, on Linden Street. (BFS.)

World-famous Phillips Exeter Academy adds its flavor to Exeter with ivy, brick, and tradition. The stately Jeremiah Smith Hall is one of the first buildings seen by those entering Exeter. Now the administration building, it was built in 1930 as the gift of alumnus Col. William Boyce Thompson, who also endowed a science building, squash court, baseball and track cages, and the Exeter Inn. (BFS.)

The Academy Building was erected in 1914 after a fire destroyed its predecessor. The architect was Ralph Adams Cram of Cram, Goodhue & Ferguson. It houses the chapel dating from when chapel attendance was mandatory and is home to the history, math, religion, and classical language programs. Two wings were added to the original structure in the 1920s and 1930s. (EHS.)

Lincoln Street School serves grades three through five and was built in 1955, with additions in 1960, 1978, and 1990. Its sister school, Main Street School, serves the needs of kindergarten and first and second grades. (BFS.)

CHAPTER 7

COMMUNITY LIFE

The Boston & Maine (B&M) Railroad made Exeter a draw during the Industrial Revolution, especially in the west end of town. The Exeter Boot and Shoe Factory was established in 1881 on Front Street. It became the Gale Shoe Factory and then the Wise Shoe Company before closing in 1972. (BFS.)

The Chemtan Company, formed in 1947, develops and sells waterproofing products for leather. The company came to Exeter in 1958, setting up shop on Hampton Road, and has been there ever since. A shipping and customer service building was added in 2015 in Lee, while research and development, manufacturing, and sales continue from the Exeter site. (BFS.)

Goodwin's of Exeter operated as a nursing home since 1935, morphing into Sunbridge Health Care and now Genesis Health Care. The facility at 8 Hampton Road is operated by a company out of Kennett Square, Pennsylvania, and takes its place alongside RiverWoods and Langdon Place to serve Exeter-area seniors with a continuum of care. (BFS.)

Gerry's Variety began as the town's depot for the B&M Railroad. The rise of the automobile reduced the railroad's use and it closed to passenger service in 1966. Service returned in 2002 with Amtrak through the efforts of local resident Bob Hall. The old building continues to be used as a variety store and lunch spot, with a standing-room-only Saturday breakfast. (BFS.)

With downtown bustling, other areas of Exeter began to develop from the overflow. Portsmouth Avenue was carved out of the wilderness, and Lincoln Street developed its own business district, with Trudel's Launderette and Mr. G's supermarket anchoring the smaller shops. Arjay True Value Hardware operates on the site of Mr. G's, while the Burnham family continues the tradition of a full-service laundry facility. (BFS.)

The Exeter Brass Works was incorporated at 10 Railroad Avenue in 1892 as part of the west end boom. Eben Folsom, Joseph Wiggin, and their employees produced fittings for water, gas, and steam along with household goods such as candlesticks. The site is still used for industrial purposes. (BFS.)

COMMUNITY LIFE

William G. "Bill" Saltonstall, the academy's ninth principal, left an impression on both the town and on private education. He is honored by the school with the William G. Saltonstall Boathouse, the center for the school's rowing program along the Squamscott River. The modern boathouse replaced several aging Water Street buildings. (BFS.)

The *Exeter News-Letter* published its first edition in 1831. It operated for a while as a daily and then as a twice-weekly, before going to its current weekly format. The company moved to this facility on Water Street in 1953 and later to a building in Stratham, before purchasing the Portsmouth Herald and moving to Portsmouth and then Pease International Tradeport. This building is currently occupied by Phillips Exeter Academy Information and Technology Services. (BFS.)

The Exeter Manufacturing Company, founded in 1829, reflected the Industrial Revolution in many ways, including letting women (and children) into the workforce and dominating the town through charismatic leadership from the Kent family. The Kents owned the mill and the Exeter Handkerchief Company, held shares in the *Exeter News-Letter*, and had the principal interest in the Exeter Banking Company. The mill and its workers, who came from all over the world, added another layer to the richness of Exeter life, and their influence is felt today. (EHS.)

Discover Thousands of Local History Books
Featuring Millions of Vintage Images

Arcadia Publishing, the leading local history publisher in the United States, is committed to making history accessible and meaningful through publishing books that celebrate and preserve the heritage of America's people and places.

Find more books like this at
www.arcadiapublishing.com

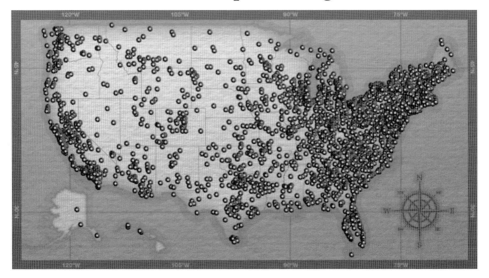

Search for your hometown history, your old stomping grounds, and even your favorite sports team.

Consistent with our mission to preserve history on a local level, this book was printed in South Carolina on American-made paper and manufactured entirely in the United States. Products carrying the accredited Forest Stewardship Council (FSC) label are printed on 100 percent FSC-certified paper.

MADE IN THE USA